Club Caxton

A Chronological List of the More Important Issues of Edward

Fitzgerald's Version

of the Rubaiyat of Omar Khayyam, and of other books, written, translated,

edited or owned by him

Club Caxton

A Chronological List of the More Important Issues of Edward Fitzgerald's Version
of the Rubaiyat of Omar Khayyam, and of other books, written, translated, edited or owned by him

ISBN/EAN: 9783337219277

Printed in Europe, USA, Canada, Australia, Japan

Cover: Foto ©Thomas Meinert / pixelio.de

More available books at **www.hansebooks.com**

Edward FitzGerald
Chronological List of His Books, Etc.

AND THIS REVIVING HERB WHOSE TENDER GREEN
FLEDGES THE RIVER-LIP ON WHICH WE LEAN—
    AH, LEAN UPON IT LIGHTLY! FOR WHO KNOWS
FROM WHAT ONCE LOVELY LIP IT SPRINGS UNSEEN!

Chronological List of the More
Important Issues of EDWARD FITZGERALD'S
*Version of the Rubaiyat of Omar Khayyam,
and of Other Books, Written, Translated,
Edited or Owned by Him; with Portraits,
Autograph Letters, etc.; and with Ana, other
Versions of the Rubaiyat, and certain Items
identified with his Name, or forming Part of
his Persian Studies*

*Exhibited by The Caxton Club (in Fine Arts
Building) Chicago, Ill. January Fourth to
January Twenty-First, 1899*

INTRODUCTION

In projecting the present Exhibition it is not so much the purpose to extol the pagan philosophy of the old Persian tentmaker, as to urge a more intimate acquaintance with the "nice little things" with which the name of Edward FitzGerald is more or less closely identified, either as editor, annotator, translator, or author. Several other books of kindred interest have been included in the Exhibition for reasons given in the notes appended to and descriptive of each. FitzGerald put his full name to only one book — Calderon's SIX DRAMAS *— and that book was withdrawn from sale shortly after its publication, and thereafter found its way into circulation mainly through private channels. Like all his other private ventures, the issue was exceedingly limited, and it is but rarely in the present day that any of these ventures appear in booksellers' catalogues.*

No money consideration ever tempted "old Fitz" — Mr. Quaritch's single honorarium of ten pounds was contributed to the fund in aid of the sufferers from the famine in Persia. As Fanny Kemble said, he "shunned notoriety as sedulously as most people seek it." He once declined to be mentioned as the author of EUPHRANOR; *and he concealed his identity with so much success that his name as translator of the* RUBAIYAT

5

was ten years in reaching his intimate friend and cor-respondent, the " Chelsea Diogenes." In 1864 — four years after the publication of his Quatrains — Mr. Ruskin addressed a letter to " The Translator of the Rubaiyat of Omar," which circled the globe for nine years before arriving at its proper destination.. But his good deeds are not suffered to lie neglected ; in America we count him happy starred—* a " Moon of our Delight who know'st no wane."

The notes to the separate issues of the Quatrains, taken mainly from FitzGerald's LETTERS, *may serve to remind us of what Mr. Edmund Gosse has said about good poetry being " almost as indestructible as diamonds. You throw it out of a window into the roar of London, it disappears in a deep brown slush, the omnibus and the growler pass over it, and by and by it turns up again somewhere uninjured, with all the pure fire lambent in its facets."*

The books in the present Exhibition which appeared prior to 1859, and with which FitzGerald's name is now identified, attracted so little attention that he was prac-tically unknown, save to the few, until after Rossetti and Swinburne found his first OMAR *in the penny box outside Quaritch's door. Indeed, in 1882, three years after the publication of the fourth issue of the* OMAR, *and only a year before FitzGerald's death, we find but one quatrain in Bartlett's* FAMILIAR QUOTATIONS, *under*

---

*Among those born in the same year (1809) with Edward FitzGerald were:

Prof. John Stuart Blackie, Mary Cowden-Clarke, Charles Darwin, W. E. Gladstone, Dr. O. W. Holmes, Lord Houghton, Abraham Lin-coln, Felix Mendelssohn, E. A. Poe, Alfred Tennyson, Robert C. Win-throp.

Omar Khayyam's name, and that sadly misquoted.
Mr. Bartlett not only took a foot out of the second line,
which he added to the third, but destroyed the sense of
the stanza into the bargain. In the ninth edition (1896)
of the QUOTATIONS, however, Mr. Bartlett atoned
in a measure for this lapse from his usual precision by
quoting the stanza correctly and adding four and a half
others. (He could have further enriched his useful
book by putting in FitzGerald's aphorism, " Taste is
the Feminine of Genius.") Today, if a new edition
of FAMILIAR QUOTATIONS were called for, it would
hardly be safe to omit a quatrain of the poem, which, in
every conceivable variety of form, has been, or is being,
put out under American imprints.* It has become the
fashion for professional and business men to point their
familiar letters with quotations from it; while the youth-
ful clerk shortens his morning jaunt to his office by
repeating his favorite stanzas; and even the gutter-mer-
chant carries a copy in his pocket.

In a little manual of this character it is not possible
to insure correctness on all points. FitzGerald himself
was very erratic, not only in his writing but in his
method of publishing, several of his books coming out in
the regular way, others being private ventures. The
first four issues of the RUBAIYAT differ each from the
other; the several issues of EUPHRANOR and SALAMAN
AND ABSAL likewise; while the three collections of LET-
TERS edited by Mr. Wright vary in many particulars;
and in neither of the collected editions do we find the
MEMOIR of Bernard Barton nor the NOTES to Selden.

*Since this Introduction was written several new Editions have
appeared, and at least two periodicals have reprinted it entire.

*Hence, a full sequence of FitzGerald's books is necessary
if one wishes to possess all he wrote.*

*The Committee has not aimed at a complete Bibli-
ography of his " Master-pieces," not even of the editions
of the* RUBAIYAT, *but the greater part of the more notable
issues of all are here, and much interesting and valuable
"ana" besides.*

The columns of the London CHRONICLE *have lately
been given over to pathetic appeals to Messrs. Macmillan
& Co. for popular editions, but as will be learned from
the present Exhibition, the enterprise of American publishers enables us to buy the book at prices ranging from
twenty-five cents to $200.00 per copy.*

*The Committee regrets that it is unable to include
a copy of* NICOLAS *among the various versions other
than that by FitzGerald; of Mr. Quilter's piracy of
the* RUBAIYAT (*1883*); *of Mr. T. J. Wise's reprint of
the first edition of the* RUBAIYAT (*1887*); *Hone's* YEAR
BOOK (*1831*), *containing* THE MEADOWS IN SPRING,
*FitzGerald's first published poem; of all the separate
issues of " Old Fitz's" "small escapades in print,"
such as* THE TWO GENERALS (*1868?*), VIRGIL'S GAR-
DEN (TEMPLE BAR, *April, 1882*), AGAMEMNON (*1865?*),
Thackeray's verses, HO, PRETTY PAGE, *set to music by
FitzGerald (*1876*),* SALAMAN AND ABSAL (*1856 edition
complete*);* and the little things reprinted by him for his
friends, such as Byron's* VERSES ON ROGERS, *Arch-
deacon Groome's* THE ONLY DARTER, *in the Suffolk
dialect (which he would have been glad to recite to Prof.
Norton " were the telephone prepared across the Atlantic*)."

*A copy has been secured and will be in the Exhibition.

The Committee would also submit that among many other items which have eluded the most diligent quest, may be mentioned FitzGerald's copy of UNDINE, *illustrated with sketches by Thackeray; the copy of Lowell's* AMONG MY BOOKS, *in which he had marked the passages he did not like and intended to show to the author sometime; the* SQUIRE-CARLYLE LETTERS, *which he (F) passed back and forth to Mr. Norton in Cambridge and Mr. Lowell in Spain; the copy of Charles Tennyson's* SONNETS *sent to Mr. Lowell; Tennyson's* POEMS CHIEFLY LYRICAL (*1830*) *bound up with* POEMS (*1833*), *with Silhouette portrait of the laureate " Done in a steamboat from Gravesend to London, Jan., 1842;" Hazlitt's copy of his* ENGLISH POETS, *with his own (H's) markings in it; the copies of Keats'* LETTERS TO FANNY BRAWNE, *and the Calderon's* DRAMAS, *sent to Mr. Lowell; the copy of Milton in which he " never could read ten lines together without stumbling at some Pedantry that tipped me at once out of Paradise, or even Hell into the Schoolroom, worse than either;" the small bunch of " Daddy" Wordsworth's* LETTERS *which he extracted and bound up from a copy of Gillie's* LIFE OF A LITERARY VETERAN *in two volumes; and the* SCRAP-BOOK *which he called "*HALF HOURS WITH THE WORST AUTHORS, *and very fine things by them." These and many of the other books FitzGerald gossiped about so learnedly and sent to his friends would add to the interest and value of such an Exhibition as the present. But perhaps we have sufficient, when considered in connection with the notes, to throw some light on his unique ideas as to the uses and abuses of books and literature. A more curious example, for instance, of the Papaverius* *order of bibliomaniac than the* BERNARD *would be hard to find. FitzGerald tells us, in a letter to Prof. Cowell (1858), that "many of the quatrains [of* OMAR] *are mashed together;" and it was by a similar licence that he "revised and decreased" a voluminous and "trashy" book. A book to him was not a "thing of beauty" but a thing of use (see notes to No. 58).*

It remains to thank Messrs. L. C. Page & Co. for courtesies cheerfully extended, and Mr. N. H. Dole for the loan of two important items in the Exhibition.

[*It is believed that the first reprint of the* RUBAIYAT OF OMAR KHAYYAM *issued on this side of the Atlantic, is that bearing the imprint, and date, of Belford Bros., Toronto, 1875.*]

THE MORE IMPORTANT SEPARATE ISSUES OF EDWARD FITZGERALD'S VERSION OF THE RUBAIYAT OF OMAR ·KHAYYAM

I RUBAIYAT OF OMAR KHAYYAM. The Astronomer-Poet of Persia. Translated into English Verse. *London: Bernard Quaritch, Castle Street, Leicester Square, 1859.*

Original paper wrappers. Pp. xiii + 21. With autographs of D. G. Rossetti and Whitley Stokes.

" Nearly the whole of this, the first edition, I sold (not being able to get more) at one penny each. Mr. FitzGerald had made me a present of about 200 copies of the 250 he had printed." So says Bernard Quaritch, in a note to the item in one of his catalogues. A copy recently sold at auction in London brought twenty pounds.

" Edward FitzGerald . . . the man whose shy audacity of diffident and daring genius has given Omar Khayyam a place forever among the greatest of English poets. That the very best of his exquisite poetry, the strongest and serenest wisdom, the sanest and most serious irony, the most piercing and the profoundest radiance of his gentle and sublime philosophy, belong as much or more to Suffolk than to Shiraz, has been, if I mistake not, an open secret for many years—'and,' as Dogberry says, 'it will go near to be thought so shortly.' Every quatrain, though it is something so much more than graceful or distinguished or elegant, is also, one may say, the sublimation of elegance, the apotheosis of distinction, the transfiguration of grace: perfection of style can go no further and rise no higher, as thought can pierce no deeper and truth can speak no plainer, than in the crowning stanza which of course would have found itself somewhat out of place beside even the gravest and the loftiest poem (Mrs. Barbauld's immortal lines on life, old age, and death) admitted or admissible into such a volume as this.

> Oh, Thou, who man of baser earth didst make,
> And who with Eden didst devise the Snake,
> For all the sin wherewith the face of man
> Is blackened, man's forgiveness give—and take!

It is of work like this that his countrymen will always think when they hear the immortal name of the workman."
—*Swinburne's Studies in Prose and Poetry.*

In a letter declining—"with many thanks"—an invitation to one of the Omar Khayyam Club Banquets, Mr. Swinburne wrote as follows:

"As to the immortal tent-maker himself, I believe I may claim to be one of his earliest English believers. It is upwards of thirty-six years since I was introduced to him by D. G. Rossetti, who had just been introduced himself—I believe, by Mr. Whitley Stokes. At that time the first and best edition of FitzGerald's wonderful version was being sold off at a penny a copy—having proved hopelessly unsaleable at the published price of one shilling.* We invested (I should think) in hardly less than sixpennyworth apiece; and on returning to the stall next day for more, found we had sent up the market to the sinfully extravagant sum of twopence—an imposition which evoked from Rossetti a fervent and impressive remonstrance. Not so very long afterwards, if I mistake not, the price of a copy was thirty shillings. It is the only edition worth having—as FitzGerald, like the ass of genius he was, cut out of later editions the crowning stanza, which is the core or kernel of the whole."

The "crowning stanza" is not missing from any "later edition" in this Exhibition.

* It was published at five shillings.

2　RUBAIYAT OF OMAR KHAYYAM. THE
　ASTRONOMER-POET OF PERSIA. Rendered
　into English Verse. *Second Edition. Lon-
　don: Bernard Quaritch, Piccadilly. 1868.*

Original paper **wrappers.** **Pp.** xviii + 30. With inscription, " W. H. Thompson from the Translator."

The second edition, of 500 copies according to Mr. Quaritch, is, in the words of Mr. Edmund Gosse, "now scarcely
less rare and no wit less interesting to the collector ;" and
a London bookseller believes it to be "rather scarcer than
the first."

"As to my own Peccadilloes in Verse, which never pre-
tend to be original, this is the story of *Rubaiyat.* I had
translated them partly for Cowell : young Parker asked me
some years ago for something for Fraser, and I gave him the
less wicked of these to use if he chose. He kept them for
two years without using : and as I saw he didn't want them
I printed some copies with Quaritch ; and, keeping some for
myself, gave him the rest. Cowell, to whom I sent a Copy,
was naturally alarmed at it ; he being a very religious Man :
nor have I given any other Copy but to George Borrow, to
whom I had once lent the Persian, and to old Donne when
he was down here the other Day, to whom I was showing a
Passage in another Book which brought my old Omar up."
　　　　　FitzGerald to W. H. Thompson, Dec. 9/61.

[LXV Second Edition.]
" If but the Vine and Love-abjuring Band
　Are in the Prophet's Paradise to stand,
　　　Alack, I doubt the Prophet's Paradise
　Were empty as the hollow of one's Hand."

[LXXVII Second Edition.]
" For let Philosopher and Doctor preach
　Of what they will, and what they will not—each
　　　Is but one Link in an eternal Chain
　That none can slip, nor break, nor over-reach."

3 RUBAIYAT OF OMAR KHAYYAM. THE
    ASTRONOMER-POET OF PERSIA.   Rendered
    into English Verse. *Third Edition. London:
    Bernard Quaritch, Piccadilly. 1872.*

Half Roxburghe. Pp. xxiv + 36.

"TO E. FITZGERALD

Old Fitz, who from your suburb grange,
    Where once I tarried for a while,
Glance at the wheeling Orb of change,
    And greet it with a kindly smile;
Whom yet I see as there you sit
    Beneath your sheltering garden-tree,
And watch your doves about you flit,
    And plant on shoulder, hand and knee,
Or on your head their rosy feet,
    As if they knew their diet spares
Whatever moved in that full sheet
    Let down to Peter at his prayers;
Who live on milk and meal and grass;
  *   *   *   *   *
            —but none can say
That Lenten fare make Lenten thought,
    Who reads your golden Eastern lay,
Than which I know no version done
    In English more divinely well;
A planet equal to the sun
    Which cast it, that large infidel
Your Omar."

                              —*Tennyson.*

Swinburne has expressed the wish that "the soul and
spirit" of Omar's thought may "be tasted in that most
exquisite English translation, sovereignly faultless in form
and colour of verse, which gives to those ignorant of the
East a relish of the treasure and a delight in the beauty of
its wisdom."

[XLVII Third Edition.]

" When You and I behind the Veil are past,
    Oh but the long long while the World shall last,
        Which of our Coming and Departure heeds
    As the SEV'N SEAS should heed a pebble-cast."

4 RUBAIYAT OF OMAR KHAYYAM; AND THE SALAMAN AND ABSAL OF JAMI: Rendered into English Verse. *Bernard Quaritch, 15 Piccadilly, London. 1879.*

Half Roxburghe. Pp. xv + 112.

This is the fourth version of the Rubaiyat. Of this version of the Salaman, FitzGerald says in one of his letters: " I took it in hand, boiled it down to three-fourths of what it originally was, and (as you see) clapt it on the back of Omar, where I still believed it would hang somewhat of a dead weight; but that was Quaritch's lookout, not mine. I have never heard any notice taken of it, but just now from you; and I believe that, say what you would, people would rather have the old Sinner alone." In this same letter [to Mr. Schutz Wilson], FitzGerald answers an inquiry as to the omission of his name from the title-page, as follows : "As to the publication of my name, I believe I could well dispense with it, were it other and better than it is. But I have some unpleasant associations with it; not the least of them being that it was borne, Christian and Surname, by a man who left College just when I went there [Edward Marlborough FitzGerald] . . . What has become of him I know not; but he, among other causes, has made me dislike my name, and made me sign myself (half in fun, of course) to my friends, as now I do to you, Sincerely yours,

(THE LAIRD OF) LITTLEGRANGE,

where I date from."

In note 25 FitzGerald tells us that "At the close of the Fasting Month, Ramazan, * * * the first Glimpse of the New Moon, * * is looked for with the utmost anxiety, and hailed with Acclamation." Then he quotes the following pretty quatrain taken elsewhere from Omar:

" Be of Good Cheer—the sullen Month will die,
And a young Moon requite us by and by :
Look how the Old one meagre, bent, and wan
With Age and Fast, is fainting from the Sky."

5 RUBAIYAT OF OMAR KHAYYAM. The
   Astronomer-Poet of Persia. Rendered
   into English Verse by Edward FitzGerald,
   with an Accompaniment of Drawings by
   Elihu Vedder. *Houghton, Mifflin and Company, Boston. 1884.*

Full brown morocco, with a design by Mr. Vedder in gold
and blind on upper cover, broad inside borders in gold, with
satin panels bearing a design by the artist which is reproduced on the satin ends. This edition is limited to one
hundred copies printed on Japan paper, of which this copy
is No. 78.

The drawings and text reproduced by the albertype
process.

Dedication—"In affectionate appreciation of her untir-
ing help and sympathy I dedicate these drawings to my
wife."

Note. "Commenced May 1883, Finished March 1884.
Roma."

In the *Century Magazine* for November, 1884, will be
found a very illuminating article by Mr. H. E. Scudder,
entitled, "Vedder's Accompaniment to the Song of Omar
Khayyam."

6 RUBAIYAT OF OMAR KHAYYAM. The
   Astronomer-Poet of Persia. Rendered
   into English Verse by Edward FitzGerald,
   with an Accompaniment of Drawings by
   Elihu Vedder. *Houghton, Mifflin and Company, Boston. 1884.*

"Ah, my Beloved, fill the Cup that clears
To-day of past Regret and future Fears:
   To-morrow!—Why, To-morrow I may be
Myself with Yesterday's Sev'n thousand Years."

7   RUBAIYAT OF OMAR KHAYYAM. The
Astronomer-Poet of Persia. Rendered
into English Verse by Edward FitzGerald.
The Grolier Club of New York. MDCCCLXXXV.

In original illuminated paper wrappers. Pp. xx + 62.

No. 55 of one hundred and fifty copies on Japan paper,
printed from type for and sold to members of the Club at
$3.00 per copy. Owing to the small number printed, the
book has rapidly risen in value, copies bringing at auction
in late years prices varying from $150 to $210.

This issue is reprinted from the edition of Bernard
Quaritch, London, 1879. The headbands are from exam-
ples in Owen Jones's Grammar of Ornament, and the cover
is from an example in Audsley's Outlines of Ornament.

> " For some we loved, the loveliest and the best
> That from his Vintage rolling Time hath prest,
>   Have drunk their Cup a Round or two before,
> And one by one crept silently to rest."

8   RUBAIYAT OF OMAR KHÁYYAM. In
English Verse. Edward FitzGerald. The
Text of the Fourth Edition, followed by
that of the First; with Notes showing the
extent of his indebtedness to the Persian
Original; and a Biographical Preface. *New
York and Boston. Houghton, Mifflin and
Company, 1888.*

Half Vellum. Pp. 124.

The Biographical Preface is signed M. K. (Michael
Kerney).

> " And we, that now make merry in the Room
> They left, and Summer dresses in new bloom,
>   Ourselves must we beneath the Couch of Earth
> Descend — ourselves to make a Couch — for whom?"

9   SELECTIONS FROM THE RUBAIYAT OF OMAR KHAYYAM.

Small quarto, paper cover. Pp. 21. One hundred copies, "printed for private circulation only among those friends whose love I prize more and more deeply as with advancing years

> The wine of life keeps oozing drop by drop,
> The leaves of life keep falling one by one."

This issue is the private venture of Mr. John L. Stoddard, the lecturer, who says in his Preface, dated Dec. 8, 1893, that "the following verses have been selected out of many which appear in the four different editions of the 'Rubaiyat of Omar Khayyam,' in order that I might have my favorite stanzas arranged by themselves, as I best love to read them. In cases where I preferred a word or line in one edition to its substitute in a later one, I have not hesitated to adopt it; but all these quatrains are the work of the great Persian poet, as interpreted and versified by Edward FitzGerald of London. . . . The thoughts expressed in the following stanzas appeal as sadly and as forcibly to us as they did to his contemporaries, though seven hundred years have rolled away since Persian roses fell upon his grave. My own enjoyment from them has been so great that, having arranged these quatrains thus in compact form, I have multiplied their copies, so that my friends may share this pleasure with me. My motive resembles that of the Duke of Buckingham, who, in the place where Anne of Austria had whispered that she loved him, let fall a precious gem, desiring that another might be happy where he himself had been."

> " Yet, much as wine has played the infidel,
> And robbed me of my robe of honor—well,
>   *I wonder often what the vintners buy*
>   *One half so precious as the stuff they sell.*

> And when like her, O Saki, thou shalt pass
> Among the guests, star-scattered on the grass,
>   And in thy joyous errand reach the spot
> Where I made one — *turn down an empty glass.*"

10 RUBAIYAT OF OMAR KHAYYAM. THE ASTRONOMER-POET OF PERSIA. Rendered into English Verse by Edward Fitz-Gerald. With an Accompaniment of Drawings by Elihu Vedder. *Houghton, Mifflin and Company, Boston, 1894.*

Crown octavo, cloth, top edges gilt. The size of this issue is one quarter that of the original folio style, and the cover and all other designs are faithful reproductions (reduced) from the originals, and approved by Mr. Vedder. One note tells us that "the Quatrains as given in this volume differ slightly in order from that adopted by FitzGerald, but the entire 101 retained by him are here included." And from another note we learn that the artist made "occasional slight changes" in FitzGerald's text, "interpolating indeed a verse of his own (number 44)," which is as follows:*

> " Listen — a moment listen! Of the same
> Poor Earth from which that Human whisper came
> The luckless Mould in which Mankind was cast
> They did compose, and call'd him by the name."

11 RUBAIYAT OF OMAR KHAYYAM. THE ASTRONOMER-POET OF PERSIA. Rendered into English Verse by Edward Fitz-Gerald. *Thomas B. Mosher, Portland, Maine.* MDCCCXCIV.

Original Japan paper boards with circuit edges. Pp. 80.

Mr. Andrew Lang's quatrains "To Omar Khayyam" (from Letters to Dead Authors) serve as a proem; and four stanzas by Justin Huntly McCarthy as L'Envoi.

> " Wise Omar, do the Southern Breezes fling
> Above your Grave, at ending of the Spring,
> The Snowdrift of the Petals of the Rose,
> The wild white Roses you were wont to sing?

* * * * * * * *

*A *lapsus calami,* which has been corrected in later issues. This is quatrain xxxviii of the Third Edition.

You were a Saint of unbelieving Days,
Liking your Life and happy in Men's Praise;
  Enough for you the Shade beneath the Bough,
Enough to watch the wild World go its Ways.

* * * * * * * *

Ages of Progress! These eight hundred Years
Hath Europe shuddered with her Hopes or Fears,
  And now! — she listens in the Wilderness
To *thee*, and half believeth what she hears!

* * * * * * * *

Ah, not from learned Peace and gay Content
Shall we of England go the way *he* went —
  The Singer of the Red Wine and the Rose —
Nay, otherwise than his our Day is spent! "

Serene he dwelt in fragrant Naishapur,
But we must wander while the Stars endure.
  He knew THE SECRET: we have none that knows,
No Man so sure as Omar once was sure! "
                              —*Andrew Lang.*

12 RUBAIYAT OF OMAR KHAYYAM.
Rendered into English Verse by Edward
FitzGerald. *Portland, Maine. Thomas B.
Mosher.* MDCCCXCV.

Original Japan paper boards with circuit edges. Pp. 125.
The following Sonnet by Mrs. Rosamund Marriott Watson on Omar Khayyam serves as a proem to this edition:

" Sayer of sooth, and Searcher of dim skies!
  Lover of Song, and Sun, and Summertide,
  For whom so many roses bloomed and died;
Tender Interpreter, most sadly wise,
Of earth's dumb, inarticulated cries!
  Time's self cannot estrange us, nor divide;
  Thy hand still beckons from the garden-side,
Through green vine-garlands, when the Winter dies.

Thy calm lips smile on us, thine eyes are wet;
  The nightingale's full song sobs all through thine,
  And thine in hers — part human, part divine!
Among the deathless gods thy place is set,
  All-wise, and drowsy with Life's mingled Wine,
Laughter and Learning, Passion and Regret."

13   RUBAIYAT OF OMAR KHAYYAM. THE ASTRONOMER-POET OF PERSIA. Rendered into English Verse by Edward FitzGerald. *Printed for E. W. Porter Company, Publishers, 100 East Fourth St., Saint Paul, Minnesota.* MDCCCXCV.

Paper boards, with cover-design, frontispiece and title-page by W. Robert Pike. Pp. 93.

Of this edition, on handmade paper, 750 copies were printed.

> " Ah, make the most of what we yet may spend,
> Before we too into the Dust descend;
>   Dust into Dust, and under Dust, to lie,
> Sans Wine, sans Song, sans Singer, and — sans End! "

14   RUBAIYAT OF OMAR KHAYYAM OF NAISHAPUR. THE ASTRONOMER POET OF PERSIA. Rendered into English Verse. *Ashendene Press.* MDCCCXCVI.

Small Quarto. Paper. Pp. xi + 48.
50 copies printed for private circulation only. This is Number 5.

"*Note.* The text here printed is not that of any one of the four editions ; but the Printer has selected from each those readings which seemed to him best, & combined them into one whole. He is aware that in so doing he cannot hope to please all ; for the lovers of Omar are sorely divided as to the merits of this or that particular turn of phrase or thought: so that he can only crave humbly the indulgence of those who may happen to disagree with his judgment."

Then follow Mrs. Rosamund Marriott Watson's sonnet, Omar Khayyam ; the following stanzas,

" La vie est vaine,
Vn pev d'amovr
Vn pev de haine,
Et pvis — bonjovr!

La vie est breve,
Vn pev d'espoir,
Vn pev de reve,
Et pvis — bonsoir ! "

a dedication "to the Memory of Edward FitzGerald ;" an address by the printer " To the gentle reader ;" FitzGerald's Introduction and the text; a Bibliography ; and the follow-ing :

"Here endeth this Book of the Rubaiyat of Omar Khayyam, translated out of the Persian into our English Tongue by Edward FitzGerald, and imprinted in this man-ner as ye may here see, by St. John Hornby & his sisters, at their private Press, Ashendene; the same having been begun & finished in the year of our Lord MDCCCXCVI., and the sixtieth of her most Gracious Majesty Victoria Brit. Regina & Ind. Imperatrix."

From the description of this edition in the Bibliography we learn that "The types used have been hand-cast from matrices given to the University of Oxford by Bishop Fell in the year 1670, and now in the possession of the Clarendon Press."

IN A COPY OF OMAR KHAYYAM.

These pearls of thought in Persian gulfs were bred,
Each softly lucent as a rounded moon;
The diver Omar plucked them from their bed,
FitzGerald strung them on an English thread.

Fit rosary for a queen, in shape and hue,
When Contemplation tells her pensive beads
Of mortal thoughts, forever old and new.
Fit for a queen? Why, surely then for you!

The moral? Where Doubt's eddies toss and twirl
Faith's slender shallop till her footing reel,
Plunge: if you find not peace beneath the whirl,
Groping, you may like Omar grasp a pearl.
        —*From James Russell Lowell's Heartsease and Rue.*

15 RUBAIYAT OF OMAR KHAYYAM. English, French, and German Translations. Comparatively arranged in accordance with the text of Edward FitzGerald's version, with further Selections, Notes, Biographies, Bibliography and other material collected and edited by Nathan Haskell Dole. Two volumes. *Printed and published by Joseph Knight Company. Boston*, MDCCCXCVI.

Cloth. Pp. clxxix + 597.

A new issue of this edition, bearing the imprint of L. C. Page & Company, and with 56 pages of additional matter and illustrations by Edmund H. Garrett and Gilbert James, came out in the present year. A set of proofs of the illustrations form part of this exhibit.

> " The Worldly Hope men set their hearts upon
> Turns Ashes — or it prospers; and anon,
>   Like Snow upon the Desert's dusty Face,
>   Lighting a little Hour or two — is gone."

16 RUBAIYAT OF OMAR KHAYYAM. THE ASTRONOMER POET OF PERSIA. Rendered into English Verse by Edward Fitz-Gerald. *Published for Will Bradley by R. H. Russell, New York (1897).*

Dark Green (stamped) paper boards. Pp. 61.

This is substantially a reprint of the Fifth Edition.

> " Some for the Glories of this World; and some
> Sigh for the Prophet's Paradise to come;
>   Ah, take the Cash, and let the Credit go,
>   Nor heed the rumble of a distant Drum!"

17 RUBAIYAT OF OMAR KHAYYAM.
THE ASTRONOMER-POET OF PERSIA. Rendered into English Verse. *London, Macmillan & Co., Limited. New York, The
Macmillan Company, 1898.*

Vellum. Pp. 112.

This is a copy of the Fifth separate issue, first reprinted
in July and October, 1890, and subsequently in July, 1891,
and February, 1893, 1894, 1895, 1896, 1897 (twice), and 1898.
On page 112 is this note by the Editor: "It must be admitted that FitzGerald took great liberties with the original
in his version of Omar Khayyam. The first stanza is
entirely his own, and in stanza XXXI of the fourth edition*
(XXXVI in the second) he has introduced two lines from
Attar (see Letters [and Literary Remains], Page 251). In
stanza LXXXI (fourth edition), writes Professor Cowell,
'There is no original for the line about the snake: I have
looked for it in vain in Nicolas; but I have always supposed
that the last line in FitzGerald's mistaken version of Quatr.
236 in Nicolas's ed., which runs thus:

'O thou who knowest the secrets of every one's mind,
Who graspest every one's hand in the hour of weakness,
O God, give me repentance and accept my excuses,
O thou who givest repentance and acceptest the excuses of every one.'

FitzGerald mistook the meaning of *giving* and *accepting*
as used here, and so invented his last line out of his own
mistake. I wrote to him about it when I was in Calcutta;
but he never cared to alter it.' "

"Earth could not answer; nor the Seas that mourn
In flowing Purple, of their Lord forlorn;
　Nor rolling Heaven, with all his Signs reveal'd,
And hidden by the sleeve of Night and Morn."

* Stanza xxxiii of Fourth Edition, which is reprinted here.

18 RUBAIYAT OF OMAR KHAYYAM.
Translated into English Verse by Edward
FitzGerald. *William Doxey, At the Sign of
the Lark, San Francisco,* (*1898*).

Issued in paper covers. Pp. 113. Opens with four quatrains by Justin Huntly McCarthy, followed by Porter Gar-
nett's poem, "Glose upon a Rubá'iy," a quotation from
M. K., and a substantial reprint of the Houghton, Mifflin
& Co. edition of the fourth and first versions. The little
volume forms No. 1 of a series called *The Lark Classics*.
This copy contains the following three quatrains, and an
inscription, by Gardner C. Teall:

" Why did'st thou say, O King of all the Wise,
  Maker of Tents, and Searcher of the Skies,—
Why did'st thou say we dust to dust descend
And lie sans Song, sans Singer and sans — End?

How can it be, the Echo of that Song
Thou sang'st in Naishapur, the Spectral Throng
All jealous of the Silence of the Tomb
Withhold or grimly smother in the Gloom!

Is't so, sweet Singer of Immortal Song?
Then powerless to right Eternal Wrong
We yet may quaff, in memory of thy Soul,
What thou did'st brew, now emptied in this Bowl."

" Oft have the footsteps of my Soul been led
    By Thee, sweet Omar, far from hum of Toil
To where the Chenar trees their plumage spread
    And tangly, wild grape-vines the thickest coil;
Where distant fields, scarce glimpst in Noon content,
    Are lush with verdure quick upon the Plough;
Where trills the Nightingale beneath the Tent
Of Heaven, uttering her soft lament;
    There have I sat with Thee and conned ere now
A Book of Verses underneath the Bough."
                                        —*Porter* **Garnett.**

19 THE RUBAIYAT OF OMAR KHAY-
YAM. THE ASTRONOMER-POET OF PER-
SIA. Rendered into English Verse by
Edward FitzGerald. The text of the
Fourth Edition followed by that of the
First, with notes showing the extent of
his indebtedness to the Persian Original.
A Biographical Preface, FitzGerald's
Sketch of the Life of Omar, and a Fore-
word by Talcott Williams.
*Philadelphia. From the Publishing House
of Henry T. Coates and Company.*
MDCCCXCVIII.

Limp leather.   Pp. lxxi + 75.

[I First Edition.]
" Awake! for Morning in the Bowl of Night
Has flung the Stone that puts the Stars to Flight;
  And Lo! the Hunter of the East has caught
The Sultan's Turret in a Noose of Light."

[I Fourth Edition.]
" Wake! For the Sun who scatter'd into flight
The Stars before him from the Field of Night,
  Drives Night along with them from Heav'n and strikes
The Sultan's Turret with a Shaft of Light."

[XI First Edition.]
" Here with a Loaf of Bread beneath the Bough,
A Flask of Wine, a Book of Verse—and Thou
  Beside me singing in the Wilderness—
And Wilderness is Paradise enow."

[XII Fourth Edition.]
" A Book of Verses underneath the Bough,
A Jug of Wine, a Loaf of Bread—and Thou
  Beside me singing in the Wilderness—
Oh, Wilderness were Paradise enow!"

20 RUBAIYAT OF OMAR KHAYYAM. THE ASTRONOMER POET OF PERSIA. Rendered into English Verse by Edward Fitz-Gerald, and into Latin by Herbert Wilson Greene, M.A., B.C.L., Fellow of Magdalen College, Oxford. *Authorized Edition. Privately printed by Nathan Haskell Dole. Boston, Mass., U. S. A.* MDCCCXCVIII. Morocco. Pp. 62.

"Of this edition have been printed nine hundred and fifty (950) copies on English handmade paper, and fifty (50) numbered copies larger format on Japan paper." (There were 100 copies printed of the original Latin version.) Mr. Dole calls this a "bilingual edition," which "is designed as a breviary for those who make a sort of cult of the Rubaiyat. Notes and introduction are superfluous: they are omitted." The text, with the Latin version in red opposite, is the one used by Mr. Wright in Letters and Literary Remains (1894).

"When in Bedfordshire I put away almost all Books except Omar Khayyam! which I could not help looking over in a Paddock covered with Buttercups and brushed by a delicious Breeze, while a dainty racing Filly of W. Browne's came startling up to wonder and snuff about me.

> 'Tempus est quo Orientis Aurâ mundus renovatur,
> Quo de fonte pluviali dulcis Imber reseratur;
>   *Musi-manus* undecumque ramos insuper splendescit;
> Jesu-spiritusque Salutaris terram pervagatur.'

"Which is to be read as Monkish Latin, like 'Dies Iræ,' etc., retaining the Italian value of the Vowels, not the Classical. You will think me a perfectly Aristophanic Old Man when I tell you how many of Omar I could not help running into such bad Latin. I should not confide such follies but to you who won't think them so, and who will be

pleased at least with my still harping on old Studies. You
would be sorry, too, to think that Omar breathes a sort of
Consolation to me! Poor Fellow; I think of him, and Oliver
Basselin, and Anacreon; lighter Shadows among the Shades,
perhaps, over which Lucretius presides so grimly."

FitzGerald to Cowell, May, 1857.

20A RUBAIYAT OF OMAR KHAYYAM.
The Astronomer-Poet of Persia. Ren-
dered into English Verse by Edward Fitz-
Gerald. Decorated by W. B. Macdougall.
*London: Macmillan & Co., Ltd. New York:
The Macmillan Company.* MDCCCXCVIII.

Small quarto, cloth, unpaged.

"This edition of the Rubaiyat is dedicated to the members
of the Omar Khayyam Club."

It is a reprint of the first edition without introduction or
notes, and is limited to 1,000 copies.

20B RUBIAYAT OF OMAR KHAYYAM,
The Astronomer-Poet of Persia.
Rendered into English Verse. First
American from the Third London Edition.
*Boston: Houghton, Mifflin and Company.
The Riverside Press, Cambridge. 1881.*

Original cloth. Pp. 78—the text being printed on only
one side of the leaf. John Wilson & Son. University Press.
This edition is now in the twenty-seventh impression.

OTHER BOOKS TRANSLATED, WRITTEN, EDITED OR ANNOTATED BY EDWARD FITZGERALD

21 THE TABLE-TALK OF JOHN SEL-
DEN, ESQ. With a Biographical Pref-
ace and Notes by S. W. Singer, Esq.
London, William Pickering, 1847.

Portrait of Selden. Pp. cxxxiv + 257 + 1 page corrigenda.

As to the *Notes*, Mr. Singer says: "Part of the following illustrations were kindly communicated to the Editor by a gentleman to whom his best thanks are due, and whom it would have afforded him great pleasure to be allowed to name." Mr. Wright quotes this remark in the Letters, and adds: "It might have been said with truth that the 'greater part' of the illustrations were contributed by the same anonymous benefactor, who was, I have very little doubt, FitzGerald himself. I have in my possession a copy of the Table Talk which he gave me about 1871 or 1872, with annotations in his own handwriting, and these are almost literally reproduced in the Notes to Singer's Edition. Of this copy FitzGerald wrote to me, 'What notes I have appended are worth nothing, I suspect; though I remember that the advice of the present Chancellor [Lord Hatherley] was asked in some cases.'"

"There is more weighty bullion sense in this book, than I ever found in the same number of pages of any uninspired writer."—*Coleridge.*

22   SELECTIONS FROM THE POEMS AND LETTERS OF BERNARD BARTON. Edited by his Daughter. *London. Hall, Virtue & Co.* MDCCCXLIX.

Cloth, Portrait of Bernard Barton, and other Illustrations. Pp. List of Subscribers, 12 leaves (unpaged) + xxxvi + 363. The "Memoir of Bernard Barton" in this volume, signed " E. F. G.," is the first published (and acknowledged) literary work by FitzGerald,* who afterwards married Barton's daughter, Lucy, the editor.† The "Memoir" has not been reprinted in either of the collected editions of FitzGerald's works, though it has been liberally "tampered with" by Mr. Edward Verrall Lucas in his book, Bernard Barton and his Friends, where it is conceded to be "a model of what such memoirs should be, for delicacy of style, justice of appreciation, and rightness of proportion."

"He had his cheerful remembrances with the old; a playful word for the young — especially with children, whom he loved and was loved by.—Or, on some summer afternoon, perhaps, at the little inn on the heath, or by the river-side — or when, after a pleasant picnic on the sea-shore, we drifted homeward up the river, while the breeze died away at sunset, and the heron, at last startled by our gliding boat, slowly rose from the ooze over which the tide was momentarily encroaching."—*From the Memoir.*
Writing to F. Tennyson, Dec. 7, '49, FitzGerald says: " I have been obliged to turn Author on the very smallest scale. My old friend Bernard Barton chose to die in the early part of this year. . . . We have made a Book out of his Letters and Poems, and published it by subscription . . . and I have been obliged to contribute a little dapper Memoir, as well as to select bits of Letters, bits of Poems, etc."

*Unless we except the poem, The Meadows in Spring, first printed in Hone's Year Book (1831).
†FitzGerald's widow died Nov. 27, 1898, aged 90 years.

23 EUPHRANOR. A Dialogue on Youth.
London, William Pickering, 1851.

In the original green cloth. Title + pp. 81.

FitzGerald's first book, of which, he said, the year following its publication, "It would be a real horror to me to be known as the writer." But later in life, after Spedding and others had praised it, he thought it "a pretty specimen of chisell'd Cherry-stone." Writing to Fanny Kemble, March 17, 1875, he said of it: "The Dialogue is a pretty thing in some respects; but disfigured by some confounded *smart* writing in parts." And again, to Lowell, April 17, 1878; "So pretty in Form, I think, and with some such pretty parts; but then some odious smart writing." Tennyson said that the description of the boat race, at the end of the book, was one of the most beautiful pieces of English prose.

24 EUPHRANOR. A May-Day Conversation at Cambridge. "Tis Forty years since."
Billings & Son, printers, Guildford. (1882).

Privately printed. Half Morocco, without regular title-page, but with much matter not in the first and second editions, especially about Tennyson, on pages 25 and 56.

In May, 1868, FitzGerald wrote to Prof. Cowell: "I had supposed that you didn't like the second Edition [of Euphranor] as well as the first; and had a suspicion myself that, though I improved it in some respects I had done more harm than good: and so I have never had the courage to look into it since I sent it to you at Oxford. Perhaps Tennyson only praised the first Edition and I don't know where to lay my hands on that . . . . I remember being anxious about it twenty years ago, because I thought it was the Truth (as if my telling it could mend the matter!): and I cannot but think that the Generation that has grown up in these twenty years has not profited by the Fifty Thousand Copies of this great work!"

25   POLONIUS: A Collection of Wise Saws and Modern Instances. *London: William Pickering. 1852.*

Original green cloth. Pp. xvi + 145.

"Few Books are duller than books of Aphorisms and Apophthegms. A Jest-book is, proverbially, no joke ; a Wit-book, perhaps, worse ; but dullest of all, probably, is the Moral-book, which this little volume pretends to be."— *From the Preface.*

"It is a collection of wise saws and modern instances, some of them his own, most of them borrowed from Bacon, Selden, Kenelm Digby, and, of the living, Carlyle and Newman, the whole graced by a charming and characteristic preface by FitzGerald himself."—*Edmund Gosse in Fortnightly Review.*

26   SIX DRAMAS OF CALDERON.   Freely translated by Edward FitzGerald. *London. William Pickering.* MDCCCLIII.

Original crimson cloth.   Pp. viii + 273 + Errata 1 leaf.

This is the only book to which Edward FitzGerald affixed his full name.

Probably not more than 250 copies were issued, and these were presently withdrawn and suppressed, because of the unfavorable reviews — one of which, in the *Athenæum*, Fitz-Gerald characterized as a "determined spit at me." "I am persuaded," he wrote to Mr. Lowell, "that, to keep life in the work (as Drama must), the translator (however inferior to his Original) must recast that original into his own Like-ness, more or less : The less like his original, so much the worse : but still, the live Dog better than the dead Lion, in Drama, I say.   As to Epic, is not Cary still the best Dante? Cowper and Pope were both men of Genius, out of my Sphere; but whose Homer still holds its own?   The elab-orately exact, or the 'teacup-time' Parody?"   FitzGerald's Calderon translations brought him the Calderon medal.

27   THE MIGHTY MAGICIAN. "SUCH STUFF AS DREAMS ARE MADE OF." Two Plays translated from Calderon. (1865.)

Privately printed, February, 1865. "I had about a hundred Copies . . . printed . . and have not had a hundred friends to give them to — poor Souls!" In gray paper wrappers; the first without title-page, the second with a half-title as follows:

"Such Stuff as Dreams are Made of."

A Drama,

Taken From

Calderon's "Vida Es Sueño."

For Calderon's Drama sufficient would seem
The title he chose for it, " Life is a Dream ; "
Two words of the motto now filch'd are enough
For the impudent mixture they label—" Such Stuff !"

John Childs and Sons, Printers. Pp. 131. Corrections on pp. 35, 37, 40, 56, 58, 59, and 75, in the translator's handwriting.

In a letter to R. C. Trench, February 25, '65, FitzGerald says:

"And I took up three sketched out Dramas, two of Calderon, and have licked the two Calderons into some sort of shape of my own, without referring to the Original. One of them goes by this Post to your Grace; and when I tell you the other is no other than your own 'Life's a Dream,' you won't wonder at my sending the present one on Trial, both done as they are in the same lawless, perhaps impudent, way. I know you would not care who did these things, so long as they were well done; but one doesn't wish to meddle, and in so free-and-easy a way, with a Great Man's Masterpieces, and utterly fail: especially when two much better men have been before one. One excuse is, that

Shelley and Dr. Trench only took parts of these plays, not caring surely—who can?—for the underplot and buffoonery which stands most in the way of the tragic Dramas. Yet I think it is as a whole, that is, the whole main Story, that these Plays are capital ; and therefore I have tried to present that whole, leaving out the rest, or nearly so ; and altogether the Thing has become so altered one way or another that I am afraid of it now it's done, and only send you one Play (the other indeed, is not done printing : neither to be published), which will be enough if it is an absurd Attempt."

Mr. Gosse says " the plays were printed separately, and more copies were distributed of the former than of the latter."

"SONG.

Who that in his hour of glory
  Walks the kingdom of the rose,
And misapprehends the story
  Which through all the garden blows;
Which the southern air who brings
It touches, and the leafy strings
  Lightly to the touch respond;
And nightingale to nightingale
  Answering a bough beyond—
Nightingale to nightingale
  Answering a bough beyond."

28 SEA WORDS AND PHRASES ALONG THE SUFFOLK COAST. Three articles from the *East Anglian* of 1868-1871 (?).

This is a set of the pages from the numbers of the *East Anglian Magazine* selected by FitzGerald, and with corrections in his handwriting. The set is enclosed in a loose wrapper marked simply "Complete."

In a letter to Mr. W. A. Wright, FitzGerald says, "My poor old Lowestoft Sea-Slang may amuse yourself to look over perhaps," and Mr. Wright did not reprint it in the Letters and Literary Remains, though Mr. Quaritch did in his collected edition (No. 35), reprinting from this copy.

29   SEA WORDS AND PHRASES ALONG
     THE SUFFOLK COAST. No. 1. Ex-
     tracted from the *East Anglian* Notes and
     Queries, January, 1869. *Lowestoft: Sam-
     uel Tymons, 60, Highstreet. 1869.*

This copy is made up of the set of the selected sheets,
with a title-page specially printed, on tinted paper, and
is bound in morocco.

30   SALAMAN AND ABSAL. AN ALLE-
     GORY. From the Persian of Jami. *Ips-
     wich. Cowell's Steam Printing Works,
     Butter Market. 1871.*

Original green cloth with leather back. Pp. xvi + 45.
This copy has the title-page and text of the second separate
edition, bound up with the "Life of Jami" (with many corrections in FitzGerald's handwriting), of the first, and was
the editorial copy used by Mr. Quaritch for his collected
edition. FitzGerald, in a letter to H. Schütz Wilson (1882),
says of the Salámán: * * * "It was the first Persian
Poem I read, with my friend Edward Cowell, near on forty
years ago: and I was so well pleased with it then (and now
think it almost the best of the Persian Poems I have read or
heard about), that I published my Version of it in 1856
(I think) with Parker of the Strand. When Parker disap-
peared, my unsold Copies, many more than of the sold, were
returned to me; some of which, if not all, I gave to little
Quaritch, who, I believe, trumpeted them off to some little
profit; and I thought no more of them."
     And again, to Prof. Norton in 1879, he says of Salámán
that it "is cut down to two-thirds of his former proportion,
and very much improved, I think. It is still in a wrong key:
Verse of Miltonic strain, unlike the simple Eastern; I remember trying that at first, but could not succeed." (See
No. 4.)

31   AGAMEMNON.   A Tragedy Taken From
      Æschylus.   *London, Bernard Quaritch, 1876.*

Half Roxburghe.   This Edition (the Second) limited to
250 copies.   Published by "my little Quaritch   *   *   *   *
at his own risk."

"Two or three years ago I had three or four of my Master-
pieces done up together for admiring Friends.   It has oc-
curred to me to send you one of these instead of the single
Dialogue [Euphranor] which I was looking in the Box for.
I think you have seen, or had, all the things but the last
[Agamemnon], which is the most impudent of all.   It was,
however, not meant for Scholars: mainly for Mrs. Kemble:
but as I can't read myself, nor expect others of my age to
read a long MS., I had it printed [in 1865] by a cheap friend
(to the bane of other Friends), and here it is."—*FitzGerald
to Pollock, 1873.*

The four lines following are said to be one of FitzGerald's
interpolations—perhaps the "one single little originality"
to which he alludes in his letter to Mr. Pollock:

> " Call not on Death, old man, that, call'd or no,
>   Comes quick; nor spend your ebbing breath on me,
>   Nor Helena: who but as arrows be
> Shot by the hidden hand behind the bow."

32   CHARLES LAMB.   A Calendar of his
      Life in Four pages.   [1878?].

The MS. additions are in FitzGerald's handwriting.

"Now I enclose you a little work of mine," writes Fitz-
Gerald to his friend Prof. Norton [1878], "which I hope does
no irreverence to the Man it talks of.   It is meant quite
otherwise.   I often got puzzled in reading Lamb's Letters,
about some Data in his Life to which the Letters referred:
so I drew up the enclosed for my own behoof, and then
thought that others might be glad of it also.   If I set down

his Miseries, and the one Failing for which those Miseries are such a Justification, I only set down what has been long and publickly known, and what, except in a Noodle's eyes, must enhance the dear Fellow's character, instead of lessening it. 'Saint Charles!' said Thackeray to me thirty years ago, putting one of C. L.'s letters* to his forehead; and old Wordsworth said of him: 'If there be a Good Man, Charles Lamb is one.'"

To "My Dear Groome," he also wrote: "By the by, I enclose a Paper of some *stepping-stones* in 'Dear Charles Lamb'—drawn up for my own use in reading his Letters, and printed, you see, for my Friends—one of my best Works; though not exact about Book Dates, which indeed one does not care for. The Paper is meant to paste in as a Flyleaf before any Volume of the Letters, as now printed."

33 THE DOWNFALL AND DEATH OF KING ŒDIPUS. A Drama in Two Parts. Chiefly taken from the Œdipus Tyrannus and Colonæus of Sophocles. The Inter-act Choruses are from Potter. (1880–1).

Half brown morocco, top edges gilded. Pages, Part I. 46, and Part II, VIII + 45. The Preface, which precedes Part II, is a letter to "My dear N—," signed "Little-Grange." The title-page is without date or place of imprint, but we learn from Mr. Edmund Gosse's Catalogue, that Part I was printed in February, 1880, and part II in the following March, both in a small private issue. The paraphrase was made for Mrs. Kemble.

In a letter to Prof. Norton, Sept. 3, '79, FitzGerald apologizes for delaying to send him the two "Sophocles Abstracts," of which he says he "would not send any but a fair MS. if

* That to Bernard Barton about Mitford's vases, December 1, 1824.—*W. A. Wright.*

I sent MS. at all; and may perhaps print it in a small way, not to publish. . . . It is positively the last of my Works! having been by me these dozen years, I believe, occasionally looked at." He had laid the Plays by after looking them over, "meaning to wait till another year to clear up some parts, if not all. Thus do my little works arrive at such form as they result in, good or bad; so as, however I may be blamed for the liberties I take with the Great, I cannot be accused of over haste in doing so, though blamed I may be for rashness in meddling with them at all."

34   READINGS IN CRABBE. "Tales of the Hall." *London, Bernard Quaritch. 1882.*

Original green cloth. Pp. xiv + 242. With a correction in the handwriting of FitzGerald. This is the editorial copy used by Mr. Quaritch for his collected edition (see No. 35), and FitzGerald's introduction here is quite different from the reprint of it in the Letters and Literary Remains, where it is dated [June, 1883]—the month and year of his death. The date of the reprint seems to have been added by the Editor, Mr. W. A. Wright.

Mr. Gosse says this selection is FitzGerald's "last literary enterprise," but some extracts from the Letters throw a fuller light on the history of this puzzling book.

To Prof. Norton, Dec., 1876:
"I wish some American Publisher would publish my Edition of Tales of the Hall, edited by means of Scissors and Paste, with a few words of plain Prose to bridge over whole tracts of bad Verse."
[These "bridges" at the breaks in the Tales have not been reprinted].

To J. R. Lowell, Oct., 1878:
"I positively meditate a Volume made up of 'Readings' from his (Crabbe's) Tales of the Hall, that is, all his better Verse connected with as few words of my own Prose as will connect it intelligibly together."

To Prof. Norton, May, 1879:

"By this post I send you my Handbook of Crabbe's Tales of the Hall, of which I am so doubtful that I do not yet care to publish it."

To J. R. Lowell, May, 1879:

"By this post I send you a bit of a Book, in which you see that I only play very second fiddle. It is not published yet, as I wait for a few friends to tell me if it be worth publishing."

To Prof. Norton, May, 1880:

"It was mainly for the Humour's sake that I made my little work: Humour . . . . which I meant to try and get a hearing for in the short Preface I had written in case the book had been published."

To Prof. Norton, March, 1883:

"The Crabbe is the same I sent you some years ago: left in sheets, except the few Copies I sent to friends. And now I have tacked to it a little Introduction, and sent some forty copies to lie on Quaritch's counter: for I do not suppose they will get further."

Hence it would appear that the book of Tales, though printed and circulated privately as early as 1879, was not regularly published, with an Introduction, until 1882 or 1883 —some copies bear the latter date. That FitzGerald contemplated, and indeed left in MS., a more comprehensive selection from his "Eternal Crabbe," must be inferred from the following:

To Fanny Kemble, Nov. 13, '79.

"Within doors, I am again at my everlasting Crabbe! doctoring his Posthumous Tales *à la mode* of those of 'The Hall,' to finish a Volume of simple 'Selections' from his other works: all which I will leave to be used, or not, whenever old Crabbe rises up again: which will not be in the Life-time of yours ever."

To W. A. Wright, May, 1883:

"The Crabbe volume would, I think, serve for an almost sufficient Selection from him, and some such Selection will have to be made, I believe, if he is to be resuscitated."

35　WORKS OF EDWARD FITZGERALD, Translator of Omar Khayyam. Reprinted from the original impressions, with some corrections derived from his own annotated copies. In two volumes. *Bernard Quaritch, London. Houghton, Mifflin & Co. Boston. 1887.*

In cloth as issued.

This edition bears a dedication which reads as follows:

"To the American people, whose early appreciation of the genius of Edward FitzGerald was the chief stimulant of that curiosity by which his name was drawn from its anonymous concealment and advanced to the position of Honour which it now holds, this Edition of his Works is dedicated by the Editor."

TABLE OF CONTENTS.

VOL. I.

Portrait of Mr. FitzGerald (by W. Griggs, after a photograph).
BIOGRAPHICAL PREFACE.
OMAR KHAYYAM'S GRAVE.
OMAR KHAYYAM'S LIFE.
　Tomb of Omar Khayyam (from a drawing by William Simpson).
OMAR KHAYYAM'S RUBAIYAT. First and Fourth Editions.
　Notes by Mr. FitzGerald.
　Notes by the Editor.
LIFE OF JAMI.
　Persian design of a game of Chugan (after a MS.).
JAMI'S SALAMAN AND ABSAL.
APPENDIX.
AGAMEMNON FROM ÆSCHYLUS.
EUPHRANOR.
POLONIUS, A COLLECTION OF WISE SAWS.
ESSAYS ON CRABBE.

VOL. II.

SIX DRAMAS OF CALDERON.
　The Painter of His Own Dishonour.
　Keep Your Own Secret.
　Gil Perez, the Gallician.
　Three Judgments at a Blow.
　The Mayor of Zalamea.
　Beware of Smooth Water.
SUFFOLK SEA PHRASES.

36 LETTERS AND LITERARY REMAINS OF EDWARD FITZGERALD. Edited by William Aldis Wright. In three volumes. *London, Macmillan and Co. 1889.*

Original red cloth. Portrait of FitzGerald in Vol. I.; Woodcut of the " Little Grange," Woodbridge, in Vol. II.; and in Vol. III the woodcut illustrating the lines:

> " Welcome, Prince of Horsemen, welcome !
> Ride a field, and strike the Ball."

TABLE OF CONTENTS.

VOL. I.

Portrait of Edward FitzGerald.
PREFACE.
LETTERS.
INDEX TO LETTERS.

VOL. II.

The "Little Grange," Woodbridge.
EUPHRANOR.
SIX DRAMAS FROM CALDERON.
THE BIRD PARLIAMENT.
THE TWO GENERALS.

VOL. III.

Persian design of a game of Chugan.
THE MIGHTY MAGICIAN.
SUCH STUFF AS DREAMS ARE MADE OF.
THE DOWNFALL AND DEATH OF KING ŒDIPUS.
    Œdipus in Thebes.
    Œdipus in Athens.
AGAMEMNON.
RUBAIYAT OF OMAR KHAYYAM.
    Notes.
    Omar Khayyam, Reprint of First Edition of.
    Variations between the Second, Third and Fourth **Editions.**
    Stanzas which appear in the Second Edition only.
    Comparative Table of Stanzas in the Four Editions.
SALAMAN AND ABSAL.
    Appendix.
BREDFIELD HALL.
CHRONOMOROS.
VIRGIL'S GARDEN.
TRANSLATION FROM PETRARCH.
PREFACE TO POLONIUS.
INTRODUCTION TO READINGS IN CRABBE.
WRITTEN BY PETRARCH IN HIS VIRGIL.

In this, the most complete collected edition of Fitz-
Gerald's Works, are several pieces published for the first
time, chief among them being Farid-Uddin Attar's "The
Bird Parliament," from which we take the following lines:

> " The Clay that I am made of once was *Man*,
> Who dying, and resolved into the same
> Obliterated Earth from which he came
> Was for the Potter dug, and chased in turn
> Through long Vicissitude of Bowl and Urn:
> But howsoever moulded, still the Pain
> Of that first mortal Anguish would retain,
> And cast, and re-cast, for a Thousand years
> Would turn the sweetest Water into Tears."

" Written by Petrarch in his Virgil

Laura, illustrious in herself, and long celebrated in my
verse, first dawned upon my eyes, while I was yet a youth,
at the Church of St. Clara in Avignon, in the year of our
Lord 1327, on the 6th of April, at daybreak. And in that
same City, in that same month of April, and that same
morning hour, of the year 1348, was that fairer light from
the light of day withdrawn, I being then at Verona, alas!
unconscious of my loss.

Her most fair and chaste body was deposited on the
evening of the day of her death in the cemetery of the
Minor Brothers. For her soul, I am persuaded (as Seneca
was of Africanus) that it is returned to the Heaven whence
it came.

I have been constrained by a kind of sad satisfaction to
inscribe this memorial in a book which the most frequently
comes under my eyes; to warn me there is nothing more to
engross me in this world, and that, the one great tie being
broken, it is time to think of quitting Babylon for ever. And
this, I trust, with the Grace of God, will not be difficult to
one who constantly and manfully contemplates the vain
anxieties, empty hopes, and unexpected issues of his fore-
gone life."

(This is the finale of the Works, apparently as designed
by FitzGerald.)

37 LETTERS OF EDWARD FITZGERALD.
In two volumes. *London. Macmillan and
Co. 1894.*

Original red cloth. Pp. **Vol. I,** xiv + 349; Vol. II, 368.
Portrait of FitzGerald in Vol. I; "Little Grange" in Vol. II.
These are the Letters separated from the Literary Remains, with some additions.

"His correspondence now reveals him, unless I am much mistaken, as one of the most pungent, individual, and picturesque of English letter-writers. Rarely do we discover a temperament so mobile under a surface so serene and sedentary; rarely so feminine a sensibility side by side with so virile an intelligence. He is moved by every breath of nature; every change of hue in earth or air affects him; and all these are reflected, as in a camera obscura, in the richly-coloured moving mirror of his letters. It will not surprise one reader of his correspondence if the name of its author should grow to be set in common parlance, beside those of Gray and Cowper for the fidelity and humanity of his addresses to his private friends."—*Edmund Gosse in Fortnightly Review.*

38 LETTERS OF EDWARD FITZGERALD
to FANNY KEMBLE, 1871–1883. Edited by WILLIAM ALDIS WRIGHT. *New
York and London. Macmillan and Co. 1895.*

Original red cloth. Pp. viii + 261.

"Of the letters which are contained in the present volume, the first eighty-five were in the possession of the late Mr. George Bentley, who took great interest in their publication in *The Temple Bar Magazine*, and was in correspondence with the Editor until within a short time of his death. The remainder were placed in the Editor's hands by Mrs. Kemble in 1883, and of these some were printed in whole or in part in FitzGerald's Letters and Literary Remains, which first appeared in 1889."—*Editor's Note.*

39 TWO LETTERS OF E. F. G.

The first letter appears to be one of those FitzGerald addressed to Mrs. W. H. Thompson, wife of the late Master of Trinity College, Cambridge, England.

The second, dated "Lowestoft; March 2/70" appears to be one of a number written to Mr. Frederick Spalding between 1865–1882. "Posh" was Edward FitzGerald's nickname for Captain Fletcher, his partner in the herring-lugger *Meum* and *Tuum*, and characterized as "a gentleman of Nature's grandest type;" "fit to be King of a Kingdom;" "who looks in his cottage like King Alfred in the Story."

Mr. Wright tells us in the Letters that FitzGerald, in the year 1871, "parted with his little yacht, the Scandal, so called, he said, because it was the staple product of Woodbridge." In September of the same year FitzGerald writes:

"I run over to Lowestoft occasionally for a few days, but do not abide there long: no longer having my dear little Ship for company. I saw her there looking very smart under her new owner ten days ago, and I felt so at home when I was once more on her Deck that — Well: I content myself with sailing on the river Deben, looking at the Crops as they grow green, yellow, russet, and are finally carried away in the red and blue Waggons with the sorrel horse."

[LXXIV First Edition.]

" Ah, Moon of my Delight who know'st no wane,
The Moon of Heav'n is rising once again:
How oft hereafter rising shall she look
Through this same Garden after me — in vain!"

40   FITZGERALD'S BOOKPLATE.   Designed by W. M. Thackeray.

It is supposed that the Angel is intended to portray Mrs. Brookfield.   In a letter to a friend, dated March 19th, 1879, FitzGerald wrote:
" Done by Thackeray one day in Coram (Joram) Street in 1842.   All wrong on her feet, so he said — I can see him now.   E. F. G."

41   PORTRAIT OF EDWARD FITZGERALD.   Etched by Costello.   1886.

Of which E. B. Cowell said, " The portrait vividly brings back my dear old friend to me."

42   WATER-COLOR DRAWING BY EDWARD FITZGERALD.

Inscribed on the back in an unknown hand, " Bredfield White House, Suffolk — painted by Edward FitzGerald. Lady Rendlesham, Mr. Manning (brother of ye Cardinal), and Mr. Robert Knipe Cobbold lived there."

Writing to Bernard Barton in 1839, FitzGerald says :
" Thank you for the picture of my dear old Bredfield, which you have secured for me: it is most welcome.   Poor Nursey [a Suffolk artist] once made me a very pretty oil sketch of it : but I gave it to Mr. Jenney.   By all means have it engraved for the pocket book : it is well worthy. Some of the tall ash trees about it used to be visible at sea : but I think their topmost branches are decayed now.   This circumstance I put in, because it will tell in your verse illustration of the view.   From the road before the lawn people used plainly to see the topmasts of the men-of-war lying in Hollesley bay during the war.   I like the idea of this : the

old English house holding up its enquiring chimneys and weathercocks (there is great physiognomy in weathercocks) toward the far-off sea, and the ships upon it.   How well I remember when we used all to be in the Nursery, and from the window see the hounds come across the lawn, my Father and Mr. Jenney in their hunting caps, etc., with their long whips — all Daguerreotyped into the mind's eye now — and that is all."

FitzGerald's Verses on his old home, "Bredfield Hall," are printed in Vol. III, — see No. 36.

[LXXII First Edition.]
"Alas, that Spring should vanish with the Rose!
That Youth's sweet-scented Manuscript should close!
The Nightingale that in the Branches sang,
Ah, whence, and whither flown again, who knows!"

ANA

43 PROF. C. E. NORTON'S REVIEWS OF NICOLAS, AND FITZGERALD'S ENGLISH VERSION (Second Edition). *North American Review.* *1869.*

Pp. 565—584. Unbound.

Prof. Norton renders thirty nine passages, in English prose, from the French of Nicolas, which, he submits, "suffer from the accumulated injuries of a double translation" and "reproduce neither the poetic form nor the style of the original verse."

At the time of writing these reviews Prof. Norton did not know the anonymous translator of the English version. But FitzGerald could not have found a more sympathetic reviewer among his friends, and as a piece of informing literary criticism that will be new to many we venture to give one of the main paragraphs here.

"Much in the English work has been simply suggested by the original. Hints supplied by Omar are enlarged; thoughts touched upon by him are completely grasped; images faintly shadowed by him, fully developed. The sequence of the Persian quatrains, depending on the rhyme and not upon the contents of the verse, admits of no progressive development of feeling and no logical continuity of thought. The poet is compelled by his form into sententiousness, into gnomic sayings, into discontinuous flashes of emotion, and finds himself obliged to recur often to the same idea, in order to present it under a new image or in a different aspect. The English Omar has not troubled himself to follow this peculiarity of his model. He has strung his quatrains together in an order which, if it fail to unite them all in a continuous and regularly developed whole, into a poem formed of the union of the separate stanzas, does at least so bind together many of them that the various portions seem like fragments of an Oriental eclogue. Moreover, a minor key of sadness, of refined melancholy, seems to recur in the English composition more frequently than in the Persian. The sentiment of the original Omar is often re-enforced by the English, is expressed in stronger, tenderer and more delicate strokes. Every now and then a note of the nineteenth century seems to mingle its tone with those of the twelfth; as if the ancient Oriental melody were reproduced on a modern European instrument. But it is very striking to see, and much more to feel, how close the thought and sentiment of the Persian poet often are to the thought and sentiment of our own day. So that in its English dress it reads like the latest and freshest expression of the perplexity and of the doubt of the generation to which we ourselves belong. There is probably nothing in the mass of English translations or reproductions of the poetry of the East to be compared with this little volume in point of value as *English* poetry. In the strength of rhythmical structure, in force of expression, in musical modulation, and in mastery of language, the external character of the verse corresponds with the still 'rarer interior qualities of imagination and of spiritual discernment which it displays."

44 EDWARD FITZGERALD. By Edmund Gosse. *Fortnightly Review, July, 1889.*

Pp. 57—70.

This article was afterwards reprinted in Mr. Gosse's book, Critical Kit-Kats, 1896.

"Who is rashly to decide what place may not finally be awarded to a man capable of such admirable feats in English prose and verse? There can be little doubt that when much contemporary clamour has died out forever, the clear note of the Nightingale of Woodbridge will still be heard from the alleys of his Persian Garden."

45 EDWARD FITZGERALD: An After-math. By Francis Hindes Groome. *Blackwoods, November, 1889.*

Pp. 615—632.

"From my bedroom-window, I could see FitzGerald's old lodgings over Berry's, where he sojourned from 1860 till 1873. The cause of his leaving them is only half told in Mr. Aldis Wright's edition of the Letters. . . . Mr. Berry, a small man, had taken to himself a second wife, a buxom widow weighing fourteen stone; and she, being very genteel, could not brook the idea of keeping a lodger. So one day, I have heard FitzGerald tell the story—came a timid rap at the door of his sitting-room, a deep 'Now, Berry, be firm,' and a mild 'Yes, my dear;' and Berry appeared on the threshold. Hesitatingly he explained that 'Mrs. Berry, you know, sir—really extremely sorry—but not been used, sir,' &c., &c. Then from the rear, a deep 'And you've got to tell him about Old Gooseberry, Berry,' a deprecatory 'Certainly, my love;' and poor Berry stammered forth, 'And I am told, sir, that you said—you said—I had long been old Berry, but now—now you should call me Old Gooseberry.'" See No. 56.

46 OMAR KHAYYAM. By Andrew Lang. *The Independent. New York.* (1890?).

In this article, which has not been reprinted, are some paraphrases by Mr. Lang, two of which follow here:

> "The Paradise they bid us fast to win
> Hath Wine and Women; is it then a sin
>   To live as we shall live in Paradise,
> And make a Heaven of Earth, ere Heaven begin?
>
> Each morn I say, tonight I will repent,
> Repent! and each night go the way I went—
>   The way of wine; but now that reigns the rose,
> Lord of Repentance, list not, but relent."

47 THE ROSE OF OMAR. By Edmund Gosse. *March 7th, 1893.*

Only 40 copies were printed, for distribution among friends, of this "Inscription for the Rose-Tree brought by Mr. W. Simpson from Omar's tomb in Naishapur, and planted today on the grave of Edward FitzGerald at Boulge."

> " Reign here, triumphant Rose from Omar's grave,
> Borne by a dervish o'er the Persian wave;
>   Reign with fresh pride, since here a heart is sleeping
> That double glory to your Master gave.
>
> Hither let many a pilgrim step be bent
> To greet the Rose re-risen in banishment;
>   Here richer crimsons may its cup be keeping
> Than brimmed it ere from Naishapur it went."

48 EDWARD FITZGERALD. By Edward Clodd. *The English Illustrated Magazine, February, 1894.*

Pp. 629—633.

"A tall sea-bronzed man, as I remember him, wearing a slouch hat, often tied on with a handkerchief, and wrapped in a big cloak, walking with shuffling gait hobnobbing with the beachmen, among whom he had his favorites, recipients of his bounty in boats and gear—everybody knew old Fitz by sight, and many called him ' Dotty.'"

49 LETTERS OF EDWARD FITZGERALD, ETC. *Edinburgh Review, October, 1894.*

Pp. 365—391.

"'What I think and know,' he [FitzGerald] said, 'of my small escapades in print' is that they are 'nice little things, some of them, which may interest a few people for a few years. But I am always a little ashamed of having made my leisure and idleness the means of putting myself forward in print, when really so much better people keep silent, having other work to do.' And this was his genuine feeling. It seemed, if one might say so, just touch-and-go whether the world ever heard of him. A shade more indolence, a shade less impetus, and the 'Nightingale of Woodbridge' might have uttered no audible note. Its absence would not only have impoverished the orchestra of modern English song, but the public would have been debarred from the privilege of his posthumous acquaintance."

50 CONCERNING A PILGRIMAGE TO THE GRAVE OF EDWARD FITZGERALD. By Edward Clodd. *London, 1894.*

Fifty copies printed for private distribution to the members of the Omar Khayyám Club. Morocco. Pp. 18.

Among other verses printed in this little book is this quatrain by Mr. Grant Allen.

" Here, on FitzGerald's grave, from Omar's tomb,
     To lay fit tribute, pilgrim singers flock;
 Long with a double fragrance let it bloom,
     This Rose of Iran on an English Stock."

Also the following Sonnet by Mr. Theodore Watts-Dunton:

" Prayer to The Winds

Hear us, ye winds! From where the North-wind strows
   Blossoms that crown ' the King of Wisdom's ' tomb,
   The trees here planted bring remembered bloom
Dreaming in seed of Love's ancestral Rose
To meadows where a braver North-wind blows
   O'er greener grass, o'er hedge-rose, may, and broom,
   And all that make East England's field-perfume
Dearer than any fragrance Persia knows:
   Hear us, ye winds, North, East, and West, and South!
   This granite covers him whose golden mouth
   Made wiser ev'n the word of Wisdom's King:
Blow softly o'er the grave of Omar's herald
   Till roses rich of Omar's dust shall spring
From richer dust of Suffolk's rare FitzGerald! "

51   CONTRIBUTIONS TOWARDS A DIC-
     TIONARY OF ENGLISH BOOK-
     COLLECTORS. Part VIII, containing
     the account of Edward FitzGerald. *Lon-
     don, Bernard Quaritch, 1896.*

Paper wrappers.   Four pages devoted to FitzGerald.

"   . . . it is true that the men whom Dibdin wor-
shipped would look upon such fellows as FitzGerald with
an eye of abhorrence and would deny to them even the
lowest rank in the roll of book-collectors. Nevertheless, on
the strength of the bookplate, which Thackeray designed
for FitzGerald, and of the fact that FitzGerald was a book-
buyer, we will give him a place in this series."
   Writing to Frederick Tennyson in August, 1843, Fitz-
Gerald says: "I had the weakest dream the other night
that ever was dreamt. I thought I saw Thomas Frognall
Dibdin — and that was all. Tell this to Alfred."

52   VERSES.   Read at the Dinner of the Omar
     Khayyam Club.   ʙʏ Austin Dobson.
     London. Printed at the Chiswick Press,
     MDCCCXCVII.

Paper. Pp. 11.

One hundred copies printed for Edmund Gosse to be
presented to the members of the Omar Khayyam Club as a
memento of his Presidency.

> " Well, Omar Khayyam wrote of Wine,
> And all of us, sometimes, must dine;
> And Omar Khayyam wrote of Roses,
> And all of us, no doubt, have noses;
> And Omar Khayyam wrote of Love,
> Which some of us are not above.
> Also, he charms to this extent,
> We don't know, always, what he meant.
> Lastly, the man's so plainly dead
> We can heap honours on his head."

53 RUBAIYAT OF OMAR KHAYYAM.

Four pages from the Illuminated Manuscript Copy (now in the possession of Lady Burne-Jones) made by the late William Morris, reproduced to accompany Mr. Walter Crane's article in *Scribner's Magazine* (July, 1897). Mr. Crane says the original is "An exquisite autograph work of William Morris's . . . which he wrote out and illuminated with his own hand, though even to this work Burne-Jones contributed a miniature, and Mr. Fairfax Murray worked out other designs in some of the borders."

> " O life that is so warm, 'twas Omar's too;
> O wine that is so red, he drank of you:
> Yet life and wine must all be put away,
> And we go sleep with Omar — yea, 'tis true."
> —*Richard Le Gallienne to the Omar Khayyam Club.*

54 IN PRAISE OF OMAR. An Address Before the Omar Khayyam Club. By the Hon. John Hay. *Portland, Thomas B. Mosher,* MDCCCXCVIII.

Original Japan paper wrapper, with a design in red reproduced from the title-page of a book of poems by Herbert P. Horne, entitled "Diversi Colores." Ten leaves, five of which are paged 1 to 9. No. 16 of 50 copies on Japan paper. A stanza by Mr. T. B. Aldrich, which faces the title-page, is printed here. Following the title is Mrs. Watson's beautiful sonnet, which cannot be printed too often, and a paragraph from the introduction to the prose version of Omar by Justin Huntly McCarthy, who also contributes L'Envoi.

> " Sultan and Slave alike have gone their way
> With Bahram Gur, but whither none may say.
> Yet he who charmed the wise at Naishapur
> Seven centuries since, still charms the wise to-day."

55　SOME SIDE-LIGHTS UPON EDWARD FITZGERALD'S POEM, "THE RUBA'- IYAT OF OMAR KHAYYAM." Being the substance of a Lecture delivered at the Grosvenor Crescent Club and Women's Institute on the 22nd March, 1898. By Edward Heron-Allen. *London. H. S. Nichols, 1898.*

In paper wrappers. Pp. 32. Mr. Heron-Allen has made A New and Literal Prose Translation of the Ruba'iyat to accompany a facsimile of the Bodleian Manuscript — the book being issued by Mr. Nichols. See No. 66.

Mr. Heron-Allen, after a careful study of the subject, has reached the conclusion that FitzGerald's poem, now so familiar to English readers as the Rubaiyat of Omar Khayyam, is the composite "result of FitzGerald's entire course of Persian studies." See note to No. 17 (Fifth Ed.)

56　TWO SUFFOLK FRIENDS. By Francis Hindes Groome. *William Blackwood and Sons, Edinburgh and London.* MDCCCXCV.

Original cloth. Pp. viii + 132.

A SUFFOLK PARSON [ARCHDEACON GROOME].
EDWARD FITZGERALD: AN AFTERMATH.

This was first published in *Blackwoods*, for November, 1889, under the title *Edward FitzGerald: An Aftermath.*

Mr. Groome tells a story of a visit his father and Fitz-Gerald made to Captain Brooke of Ufford, the possessor of one of the finest private libraries in England. "The drawing-room there had been newly refurnished, and FitzGerald sat himself down on an amber satin couch. Presently a black stream was seen trickling over it. It came from a penny bottle of ink, which FitzGerald had bought in Woodbridge and put in a tail-pocket." See No. 45.

57 HUETIANA, OU PENSEES DIVERSES DE M. HUET, EVEQUE D'AVRANCHES. *Amsterdam, 1723.*

Twelve mo, in old calf. With a note of two pages in the handwriting of FitzGerald, extracted from Sainte-Beuve, and the Bookplate of FitzGerald; likewise the bookplate of the late Charles Keene, who has written within the cover, "Given to me by E. FitzGerald. C. S. K."

58 RETROSPECTIONS OF THE STAGE. By the late John Bernard, Manager of the American Theatres, and formerly Secretary of the Beef-Steak Club. *London. Henry Colburn and Richard Bentley. New Burlington St. 1830.*

Originally in two volumes, but reduced to one by a system of clipping and pasting and transcribing original with Edward FitzGerald, the former owner of the book, whose bookplate, designed by Thackeray, is on the inside of upper cover.

To his friend W. B. Donne, FitzGerald wrote in 1865, "I have been reading and reducing to one volume from two (*more meo*), a trashy Book, 'Bernard's Recollections (*sic*) of the Stage,' with some good recollections of the Old Actors, up to Macklin and Garrick.   But, of all people's one can't trust Actor's Stories."   And, as indicating his preferences, FitzGerald wrote to Prof. Norton in one of his letters (1883): " I got our Woodbridge Bookseller to enquire for your Mr. Child's Ballad-book; but could only hear, and indeed be shown a specimen, of a large Quarto Edition, *de luxe* I believe, and would not meddle with that.   I do not love any unwieldy Book, even a Dictionary ; and I believe that I am contented enough with such Knowledge as I have of the old Ballads in many a handy Edition.   Not but I admire Mr. Child for such an undertaking as his ; but I think his Book will be more for Great Libraries, Public or Private, than for my scanty Shelves at my age of seventy-five.   I have already given away to Friends all that I had of any rarity or value, especially if over octavo."

Mr. John Loder, the Bookseller alluded to, gave to Mr. Francis Hindes Groome, some years ago, a book which the latter describes as "'made up,' like so many others, by Fitz-Gerald, and comprising this one, three French plays, a privately printed article on Moore, and the first edition of 'A Little Dinner at Timmins's.' "

OTHER VERSIONS OF THE RUBAIYAT, ETC., WITH CERTAIN BOOKS WHICH FORMED PART OF FITZGER- ALD'S PERSIAN STUDIES

59 DIE LIEDER UND SPRÜCHE DES OMAR CHAJJAM. Verdeutscht Durch Friedrich Bodenstedt. *Breslau, 1881. Schletter'sche Buchhandlung (E. Franck).*

Small octavo, cloth. Pp. **xxii + 217.** Printed in **three** colors — black, red and blue.

Bodenstedt claims to give "a fairer idea of Omar than is to be found in FitzGerald, who, he thinks, scarcely does justice to the old Persian's 'Gottlicher Humor.'"

60 THE STROPHES OF OMAR KHAY- YAM. Translated by John Leslie **Gar-** ner, With an Introduction and Notes. *Milwaukee. The Corbitt & Skidmore Co. 1888.*

Square 12mo. Cloth. Pp. xii + 76.

"While **Omar's** fatalism and indifference may to many seem **pernicious,** thrusting themselves forward in such a manner that they cannot **be** overlooked, the effect of the whole is, as Mr. FitzGerald says, more apt to move sorrow than anger towards the old Tent-maker."

—From the Introduction.

61 RUBAIYAT OF OMAR KHAYYAM.
Translated by Justin Huntly McCarthy,
M.P. *London. David Nutt.* MDCCCLXXXIX.

Pages lxii + clvi. No 19 of sixty copies printed on large
(Japan) paper.

"Keats once entreated some traveller who was going to
the East, to take a copy of 'Endymion' with him, and when
he came to the great Sahara, to cast the volume from him
with all his force far away into the yellow waves of sand.
It was a delicious fantastic wish, that the loveliest poem of
our later English speech should lie and drift in the remote
Sahara and be covered at last in the sand that has engulfed
so many precious things, but none more precious, caravans,
and gold, and tissues, and fair slaves, and the chiefs of
mighty clans. If I might frame a wish in distant emulation,
I would choose that some wanderer to the East, some
Burton, some Kinglake, some Warburton, might carry this
little book in his saddle-bags, and ride through Khorassan
till he came to Nishapur, and cast it down in the dust
before the tomb of Omar Khayyam."
                              —*Justin Huntly McCarthy.*

62 RUBAIYAT OF OMAR KHAYYAM.
A PARAPHRASE FROM SEVERAL LITERAL
TRANSLATIONS. By Richard Le Gallienne.
New York. John Lane, The Bodley Head.
MDCCCXCVII.

Octavo. Paper boards. Pp. 107. The issue in this form
limited to 1250 copies.

"Probably the original rose of Omar was, so to speak
never a rose at all, but only petals toward the making of a
rose; and perhaps FitzGerald did not so much bring Omar's
rose to bloom again, as to make it bloom for the first time.

The petals came from Persia, but it was an English Magician who charmed them into a living rose."
—*From Mr. Le Gallienne's Note to the Reader.*

63 THE QUATRAINS OF OMAR KHEY-
YAM OF NISHAPOUR, Now first completely done into English Verse from the
Persian, in accordance with the Original
Forms, with a Biographical and Critical
Introduction, by John Payne, Author of
"The Mask of Shadows and Other Poems,"
&c., &c., and Translator of "The Book of
the Thousand Nights and One Night," &c.,
&c. *London:* MDCCCXCVIII: *Printed for the
Villon Society by Private Subscription and
for Private Circulation only.*

Bound in Vellum, Pp. lxxxi + 206 + one page of advertisements. No. 3 of 750 copies on handmade paper. There
are also 75 copies on large paper. Mr. Payne gives 845
quatrains, of which No. 83 is as follows:

"Like water in the river, like wind on wold, for aye
Of thine and my existence gone is another day:
Of two days and their canker I never yet did reck —
The day that's still unmorrowed, the day that's past away!"

In the announcement of Mr. Payne's book, we are told
that "No complete or adequate translation of the Rubaiyat
or Quatrains of the great poet of twelfth century Persia has
yet appeared. Mr. FitzGerald's elegant paraphrase of a
small portion (about one-eighth of the whole), although a
charming poem which will always, on its own merits, retain
its place in English literature, is so exceedingly loose, and
often indeed so extravagantly wide of the mark, that it

affords practically no idea of the original; and the other translations which exist, whilst a little more exact, are wholly destitute of the poetical charm which makes the earlier version, with all its shortcomings, dear to the lover of poetry."

64   THE STANZAS OF OMAR KHAYYAM. Translated from the Persian by John Leslie Garner.   Second Edition with Introduction and Notes.   MDCCCXCVIII.   *Published by Henry T. Coates and Company.   Philadelphia.*

Limp leather.   Pp. 79.

> " The herald of the morn, in lusty tone,
>   Loud greets the dawn upon her golden throne,
>   Again proclaiming to a slumbering world:
>   Another night beyond recall has flown."

65   THE QUATRAINS OF OMAR KHAY- YAM.   THE PERSIAN TEXT WITH AN ENG- LISH VERSE TRANSLATION.   By E. H. Whinfield, M.A., Late of the Bengal Civil Service.   *London: Trübner & Co., Ludgate Hill.   1883.*

Original cloth.   Pp. xxxii + 335.   First Edition is dated 1882, and is without the Persian text.

> " A potter at his work I chanced to see,
>   Pounding some earth and shreds of pottery;
>   I looked with eyes of insight, and methought
>   'Twas Adam's dust with which he made so free!
>
> No longer hug your grief and vain despair,
>   But in this unjust world be just and fair;
>   And since the substance of the world is naught,
>   Think *you* are naught, and so shake off dull care! "

66 THE RUBA'IYAT OF OMAR KHAY-
YAM. Being a Facsimile of the Manu-
script in the Bodleian Library at Oxford,
With a Transcript into modern Persian
Characters, Translated with an introduc-
tion and notes, and a bibliography by
Edward Heron-Allen. [Here follow three
lines of Persian text]. *London.* **H. S.**
Nichols, Ltd., 39 Charing Cross Road, **W. C.**
MDCCCXCVIII.

Original cloth. Pp. xlii + 320.

The printed title-page is preceded by an engraved title
in black and red capitals, the wording being slightly
abridged. A Second Edition, carefully revised and con-
siderably enlarged, bears the imprint of L. C. Page &
Company, Boston.

67 THE GULISTAN; OR, ROSE GARDEN,
    OF SHEKH MUSLIHU'D-DIN SADI
    OF SHIRAZ. Translated for the first
    time into Prose and Verse, with an In-
    troductory Preface, and a Life of the
    Author, from the Atish Kadah. By Ed-
    ward B. Eastwick, F.R.S., M.R.A.S., of
    Merton College, Oxford, Member of the
    Asiatic Societies of Paris and Bombay;
    and Professor of Oriental Languages and
    Librarian in the East India College,
    Haileybury. *Hertford. Printed and Pub-
    lished by Stephen Austin, Bookseller to the
    East India College.* MDCCCLII.

Octavo.   Full morocco.   Pp. xxx + 309 + 1 page of
Errata.

This book, in the original and in the present translation,
formed part of FitzGerald's Persian Studies; and some of
its passages, Mr. Heron-Allen assures us, are echoed in his
Version of the Rubaiyat.

In 1853 FitzGerald ordered a copy of Eastwick's Gulistan:
"for I believe I shall potter out so much Persian," he said
to Mr. Cowell. And in 1857 he wrote to Mr. Cowell, "yesterday I bought at that shop in the Narrow Passage at the End
of Oxford Street a very handsome small Folio MS. of Sadi's
Bostan for 10s." Again to Mr. Cowell, in 1868, "I wish you
would have Semelet's Gulistan which I have. You know I
never cared for Sadi."

> " In this fond hope, dear life, alas! has waned:
>   That my heart's wish might not be wished in vain
>   Hope, long delayed, is granted. Have I gained
>   Aught? — Nay. Life spent returns not back again."

68 NOTE SUR LES RUBÂ'IYÂT DE 'OMAR KHAÏYÂM. Par M. Garcin De Tassy, Membre De L'Institut. *Paris. Imprimerie Impériale.* MDCCCLVII.

In original paper cover as issued. Pp. 11.

To Mrs. E. B. Cowell, FitzGerald wrote, April 22, 1857, as follows:

" Now this morning comes a second Letter from Garcin de Tassy, saying that his first note about Omar Khayyam was 'in haste:' that he has read some of the Tetrastichs which he finds not very difficult ; some difficulties which are probably errors of the ' copist;' and he proposes his writing an Article in the Journal Asiatique on it in which he will ' honourably mention' E. B. C. and E. F. G. I now write to deprecate all this: putting it on the ground (and a fair one) that we do not yet know enough of the matter : that I do not wish E. B. C. to be made answerable for errors which E. F. G. (the 'copist') may have made: and that E. F. G. neither merits nor desires any honourable mention as a Persian Scholar: being none. Tell E. B. C. that I have used his name with all caution, referring de Tassy to Vararuchi, etc. But these Frenchmen are so self-content and superficial, one never knows how they will take up anything."

69 THE ROSE GARDEN OF PERSIA. By Louisa Stuart Costello. *London. John Slark. 1888.*

Octavo, cloth. Pp. xvi + 193.

This book contains no reference to FitzGerald, but it does contain a short note on Omar Khiam, who "may be called the Voltaire of Persia," and some verses from his Rubajat, of which the following is a sample :

> " Ye who seek for pious fame,
>   And that light should gild your name,
>   Be this duty ne'er forgot,
>   Love your neighbour — harm him not."

It is only fair to add, however, that the Author of "The Rose Garden of Persia" died in 1870, and the present copy is one of a "New Edition" of her book — which seems to have been unknown to FitzGerald, though it was first published in 1845. Yet FitzGerald may have had the book in mind when he wrote to Mrs. Cowell (1877), "I never see any Paper but my old Athenæum, which, by the way, now tells me of some Lady's Edition of Omar which is to discover all my Errors and Perversions. So this will very likely turn the little Wind that blew my little Skiff on."

70 GHAZELS FROM THE DIVAN OF HAFIZ. Done into English by Justin Huntly McCarthy. *London. Published by David Nutt. New York. C. Scribner's Sons.* MDCCCXCIII.

Paper boards. Pp. vii + 152.

This little book, in the original and in other translations than the present, is often referred to by FitzGerald, who says, in one of his letters, " Hafiz and old Omar Khayyam ring like true metal." In his dedication to Mr. William Ernest Henley, Mr. McCarthy says: "To some the head of Omar is circled with a halo of mysticism, while others see only the vine-leaves in his hair. You will decide for yourself, as you please, whether the Beloved is Spirit or very Flesh, whether the wine is the Blood of the Grape or the Ichor of Doctrine. All that is certain is, that Hafiz was born in the dawn of the fourteenth century and that he died in its dusk, and that between the date of his birth and the date of his death he wrote some songs which have filled the world with their music."

" Grieve not; if the springtide of life should once more mount the throne of the garden, thou wilt soon, O singer of the night, see above thy head a curtain of roses."

71 IN A PERSIAN GARDEN. A Song-
Cycle for Four Solo Voices (Soprano,
Contralto, Tenor and Bass). With Piano-
forte Accompaniment. The words selected from the Rubaiyat of Omar Khayyam (FitzGerald's Translation). The
Music composed by Liza Lehmann. *London: Metzler & Co., Lt'd. New York:
G. Schirmer.* (*1896*).

Quarto, paper. Pp. 8 + 76.
The twenty-eight quatrains and four couplets making up
the book have been slightly modified as to the words, and
transposed as to the order, to suit the requirement of the
music.

PRINTED BY R. R. DONNELLEY
AND SONS COMPANY AT THE
LAKESIDE PRESS, CHICAGO, ILL.

www.ingramcontent.com/pod-product-compliance
Lightning Source LLC
Chambersburg PA
CBHW021531270326
41930CB00008B/1200